Jesus
Walks on Water

Bibleworld Books contains stories adapted
from the *Contemporary English Version* of the Bible.
Each book is designed to provide early readers with a text
adapted from Scripture in a form and manner that helps them
develop their reading skills and introduce them to the narrative of the Bible.

Adapted from:
Mission Literacy Readers Level 1 & 2
© 2008 American Bible Society
Used by permission.

Jesus Walks on Water is based on Matthew 14:22-33

ISBN: 978-0-901518-75-0

Series 1: Book 4

Illustrated by Graeme Hewitson

© 2017 The Scottish Bible Society (Formerly The National Bible Society of Scotland).
Company number SC238687, Scottish Charity SC010767
All rights reserved.

The Scottish Bible Society
7 Hampton Terrace, Edinburgh. EH12 5XU
www.scottishbiblesociety.org

Series 1: Who was Jesus

Jesus and the Storm
Jesus Heals a Man
Jesus Feeds a Crowd
Jesus Walks on the Water

Bibleworld Books provides three full session outlines to accompany each story book with games and activities designed to raise each child's learning potential.

Available for free download at www.bibleworld.co.uk

All day long, Jesus had been talking to crowds of people.

His disciples had been helping him.

It was getting late, and they were all so tired.

"Go get in the boat and go back across the lake," Jesus told them. "I will stay here."

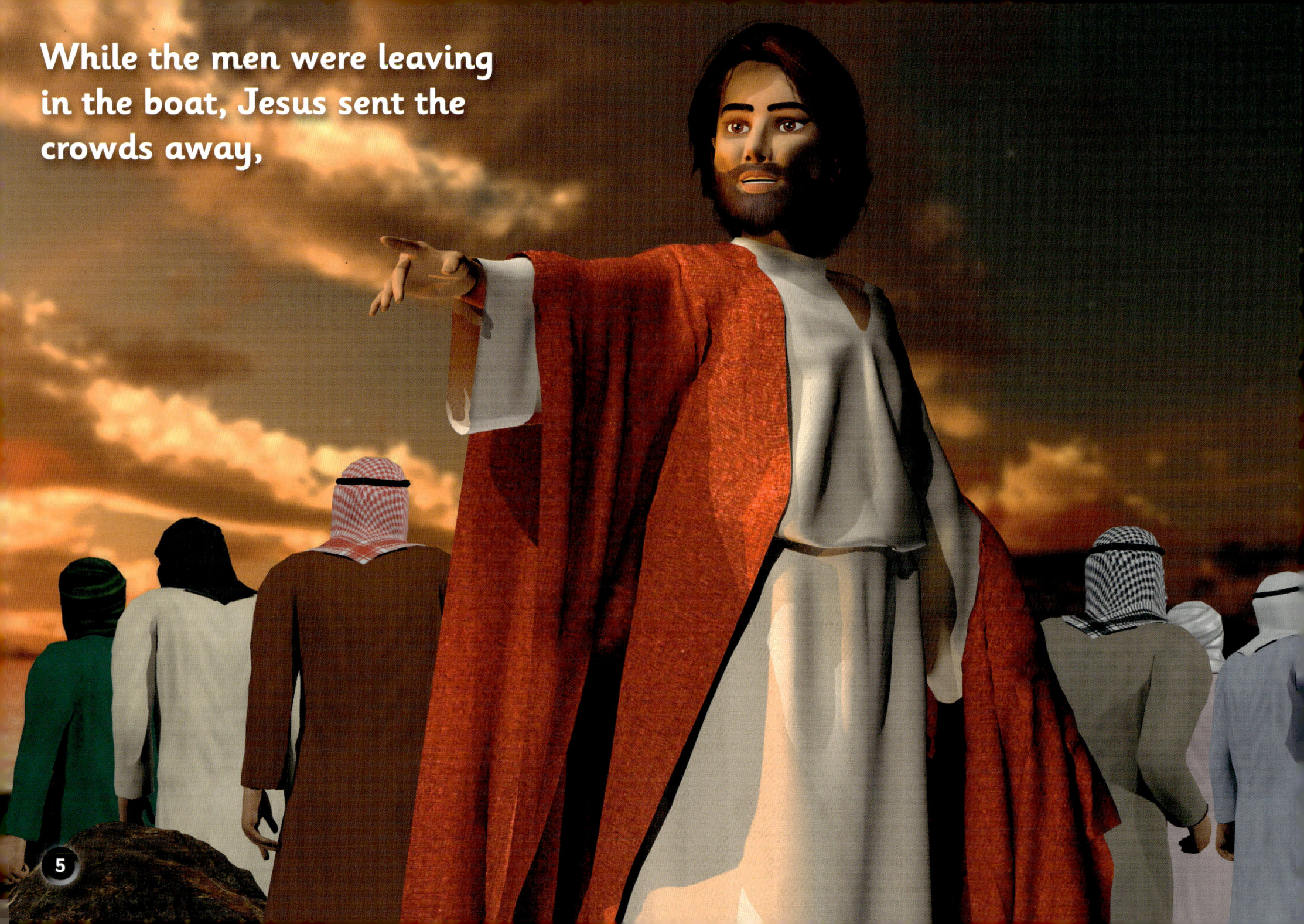

While the men were leaving in the boat, Jesus sent the crowds away,

and then he went to pray.

By now the boat was far out on the water, far away from the land.

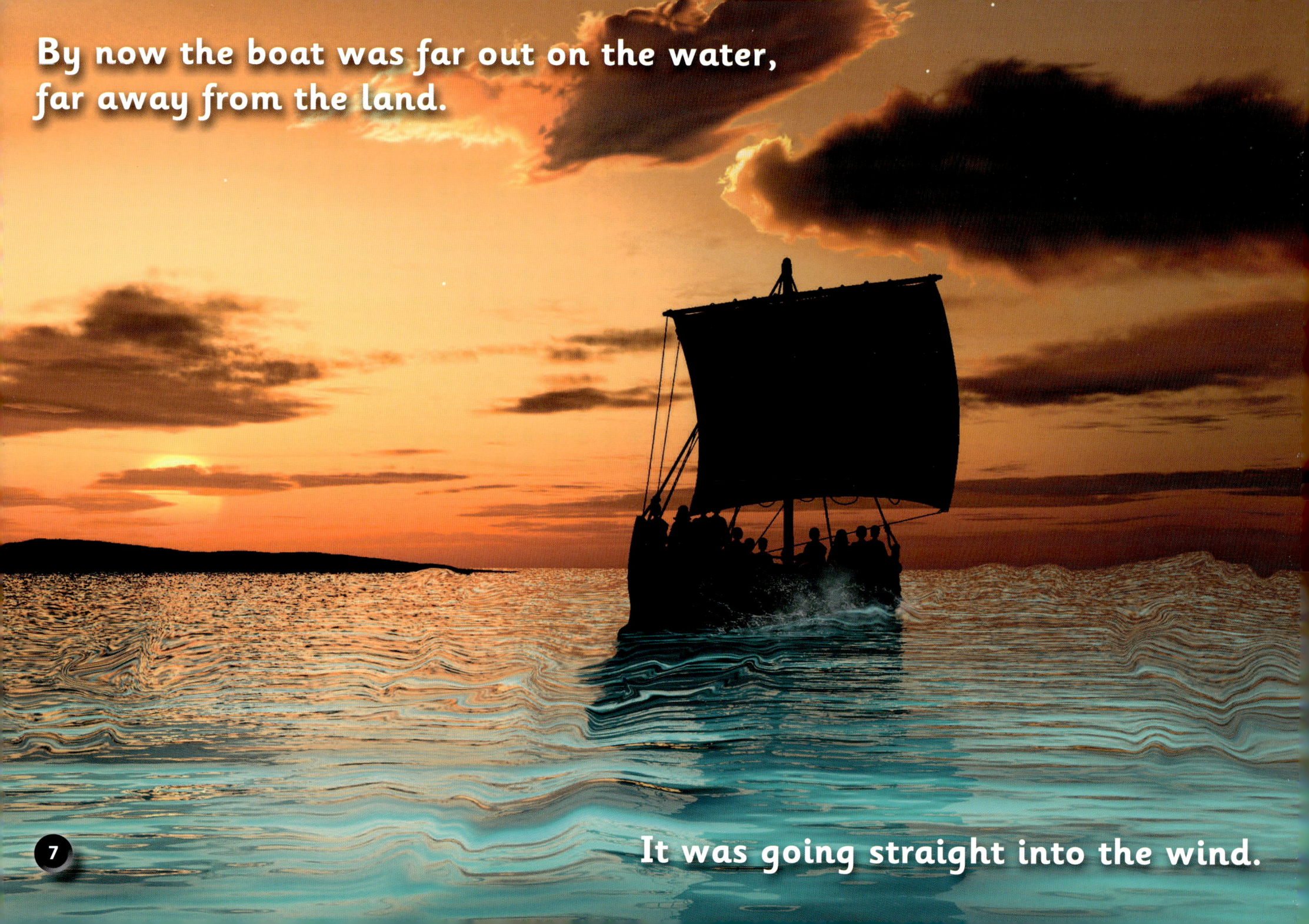

It was going straight into the wind.

And then suddenly they saw Jesus, walking on the water!

"If you are Jesus," Peter yelled, "tell me to come to you!"

"Come on, then!" Jesus said.

Jesus reached out and took hold of Peter.

He helped him stay on top of the water.

"Peter," he asked, "where is your faith? Why did you get scared?"

As Jesus and Peter got into the boat, the wind stopped blowing!